Speed Reading

Read Faster, Save Time and Accomplish More

By Jonah Udell

as a result of the use of information contained within this document, including, but not limited to, —errors, omissions, or inaccuracies.

Table of Contents

Introduction

We live in a day and age when learning a lot of things quickly is important for academic, personal, and career success. We have to make the most out of our limited time by optimizing productivity and the only way to do that is continuous learning.

But as more and more demands are being placed on our limited time, energy and resources, we all need to find a way to learn more and more things in less time. And one of the best ways to do that is through learning how to speed read.

In this book, you'll learn what speed reading is and isn't, the benefits of learning how to speed read and, more importantly, important principles and techniques for speed reading. By the end of this book, you'll have enough information to start ramping up your reading speed. So, what are you waiting for? Turn the page and let's begin!

Chapter 1: Lets Get Speed Reading

The term "speed reading" refers to a method of reading that lets a person read at a significantly faster pace. Speed reading can be done by selectively reading specific phrases or words that are related to the reading material, via skimming or through other speed reading techniques that you will discover later in the book.

While there is an inverse correlation between reading speed and comprehension level, i.e., optimal comprehension is achieved at lower reading speeds, you can still benefit much from learning how to speed read. Some of the benefits you can experience when you learn how to speed read include:

1) **Spend Less Time Reading and More Time Learning:** When you're able to speed-read, you won't take as much time as usual just to understand the essential points of what you're trying to read. This means you'll be able to learn more things given the same length of time and you'll be able to get more things done.

2) **Greater Mental Focus:** A great chunk of speed reading is focusing on the words you're reading on a given body of text as well as their groupings and your reading pace. As you learn to speed read, you'll inadvertently

learn to focus better and become more mindful of what you're doing.

3) **Better Memory:** The ability to read more with relatively good comprehension level can help you memorize and retain more things in your mind compared to reading at your current, regular pace. The more you can read and comprehend in a given length of time, the more you'll be able to store in your memory.

4) **Improved Problem-Solving Abilities:** When you're able to read and comprehend more within a specific length of time compared to what you can do at the moment, you'll be able to learn more hacks that can help you solve everyday challenges.

5) **Higher Grades:** If you're a student, being able to read and comprehend more in a given length of time can help you understand more of your school's lessons better. This can help you get higher grades when it comes to taking your exams.

6) **Improved Decision-Making Abilities:** Finally, when you're able to read and learn more new and useful things, you can gain more useful information and increase your stock knowledge. The more you have in your stock knowledge, the more decision-making options you can have, which can help you make wiser decisions in the future.

What It Is and What It's Not

Before proceeding further, you'll need to get the skinny on speed reading so you can appreciate it for what it really is and avoid unrealistic expectations about it.

Speed reading is a very useful skill that can help you learn the main points or general ideas presented in a given body of text, especially when you're under time pressure. For example, your boss' boss suddenly asks you to present the final internal audit report to the company's Board of Directors after lunch, in lieu of your boss who had to call in sick due to the flu.

Unless you're the one who prepared the report, you'll have limited time to digest everything in the report. But because most presentations to top management are usually high-level, meaning they only need to understand the general benefits and implications of what's being presented, you can focus on identifying and understanding the main points and sub-points of said report within the limited hours you're given. For this, speed reading is perfect. ps... This is why I personally learnt how to speed read

Another situation similar to the aforementioned one where speed reading can prove to be very useful is writing meaningful content, whether it's for a blog, a book, or a report.

Freelance writers who need to meet specific word-count quotas and deadlines on a daily and weekly basis are some of the best speed readers around. Often times, they write on a wide range of topics and genres, many of which are unfamiliar to them. The only way they can crank out the required number of word contents within limited periods of time is by being able to quickly get the general ideas out of the content they're able to research.

Speed reading isn't a topic mastery tool. As mentioned earlier, there's an inverse correlation between optimal reading comprehension and reading speed. This means if you want a very deep understanding or complete mastery of a given topic, you can't afford to just understand the main ideas of related contents. You'll need to slow down enough to process every bit of information in the texts you read.

A good example would be taking computer programming classes. Speed reading can help you prepare for your classes by giving you a good understanding of the general ideas that will be discussed in the classes, which can serve as useful learning anchors or wireframes. These learning anchors or wireframes can help you relate new and unfamiliar information to something you already understand, which help you understand them better.

Mastery requires understanding nuances of specific terminologies and concepts. The word "iteration" is a fairly complex term used in software development, which a student like you who's just learning computer programming may not completely understand. When you come across this term in speed reading, you can't afford to just continue reading. Either you'll have to stop and research what the term means or highlight it so you can research what it means afterward. Regardless of your choice, you'll have to rely on something more than speed reading to master computer programming.

Now that you understand what speed reading is and is not, you'll be in a very good position to know when to use it for your optimal learning results.

Chapter 2: The Power of Your Brain

Before we get into the details of speed reading, it's important to understand how the brain works during normal and speed reading, and how it stores information. This will help you to better use the speed reading techniques you'll learn later and to appreciate them more. I promised a "No Fluff" guide and that's what I plan to deliver. I have only included information I deem relevant to understand why the techniques work. I believe knowing this information will help you see why practising these strange techniques can work once you understand how the brain reacts to them.

How the Brain Processes Normal Reading

When a person reads printed materials, there are 3 ways by which the brain processes information obtained from such materials. These are:

1) **Visual Information Processing:** In this step, the eyes visually process the information from the words (reading) and the brain processes the images of the words. The brain recognizes and registers these images under visual information processing.

2) **Acoustical Information Processing:** During this step, the brain records the visual information it has processed as an acoustic

message or voice in the language that it understands, e.g., English, Japanese, Spanish, etc. During acoustical information processing, a person "hears" the processed words in the brain and reads words exactly as they sound when pronounced. Here, the brain acoustically encodes the information that was processed visually earlier. This can sometimes be acoustically processed in the voice of the author if this is someone you know or admire as if they are actually speaking directly to you.

3) **Meaning or Semantic Processing:** In this final reading-information processing step, the brain analyzes visually and acoustically-processed information in the familiar language / voice. The brain also extracts the meaning of such information in this stage, which allows it to obtain significant information from the words read.

How the Brain Functions During Speed Reading

As mentioned earlier, a person who uses speed reading can read and learn significantly more compared to regular-paced reading. Anybody can learn this skill and can master it by practicing consistently. When a person speed reads, that person can adjust how the brain functions while reading. Basically, speed reading improves or optimizes the human brain's information processing capacities related to reading.

When a person reads normally or at regular pace, that person can read anywhere from 180 to 230 words every minute. A person who speed reads can read as much as 900 words every minute!

How does the human brain do that? By employing specific speed reading techniques that allow it to adjust its visual and acoustical information processes accordingly. You will learn these techniques in the succeeding chapters.

How the Brain Memorizes Information

We can define memory as an ongoing process that recruits many areas of the body, including the brain. Contrary to what many people think, memory isn't a physical part or organ in the body like the brain or the kidneys.

The term "memories" refer to mental reports or files of things that have happened in the past, which includes our recollections of past experiences. Memories start with the senses, which are the means by which we experience things, e.g., sight, sound, touch, taste, and smell.

Our brain chooses which among the many different experience-related information we obtain on a daily basis will be saved as memories. If the brain doesn't filter which information should be saved, it will overload itself and will not be able to function at all. That's why the brain has to selectively save information as memories.

The hippocampus is the primary part of the brain that processes memories. Many experts believe that information that the hippocampus processes is stored in different areas of the brain's cerebral cortex, a.k.a., the "gray matter." This is how your brain will retain the important information when you speed read.

When the brain accumulates memories, it also determines how important stored memories are. To avoid being overloaded, the brain continuously filters and prioritizes processed information. The brain places information it deems needed for a brief period of time, e.g., a phone number for immediate and one-time dialing, in a "folder" called short-term memory.

The mental folder called short-term memory has very limited storage space. Experts believe that most people can only store up to a maximum of 7 items in short-term memory for no longer than 30 seconds. One of the ways to extend the stay of information in short-term memory is repetition.

The brain transfers the most important pieces of information from short-term to long-term memory. Intentional or unintentional repetition can make the brain assign a great degree of importance to specific items in short-term memory and compel the brain to shuttle it to the long-term memory mental folder. The degree of emotional impact specific experiences provide can influence the degree of importance that the brain will assign to them, which eventually determines whether or not they'll be transferred to the long-term memory folder.

The good news is that long-term memory isn't constrained by the same storage space limitations as short-term memory is. Many scientists think that the long-term memory has neither limits when it comes to the number of memories stored nor the length of time memories are stored. Think about it: some of your most unforgettable memories are those from many years ago, including childhood ones.

The Mind's Ability to Absorb Imagery and Ideas

The mind absorbs and retains information in different ways. And when it comes to memory retention, there's a reason for the saying that a picture paints a thousand words. Images help us learn something better, grab our focus and attention much easier, explain relatively complex ideas better, and inspire us.

But why do we respond much better to visual stimuli compared to others? The simplest answer would be that we're visual beings, with a great chunk of our brain focused on visual processing. Compared to other kinds of information, our brain processes visual information (images) at a much faster rate. Consider the following:

1) **Read this sentence;** "Stephen Curry made the game winning 3-point shot for the Golden State Warriors against the Houston Rockets." and

2) Look at a picture of Stephen Curry launching a 3-point shot with James Harden on his face and a picture of the game clock with just a second remaining.

If you go with number 1, it'll take you at least 2 to 3 seconds to process and understand the information. But with number 2, it'll just take you a second. That's how fast visual information processing is.

When you read memory improvement books, one of the most recommended tactics for easily committing a specific piece of information to long-term memory is by painting an absurd picture of it in the mind. Why? According to memory experts, the crazier the image is, the more it'll stand out and the harder it'll be to forget it.

I hope you can see how powerful your brain really is and how it will easily store the information delivered to it through reading and how, with a bit of practice, you can speed this process up without losing any of the required information.

Chapter 3: Determine Your Reading Speed

Now that you know how powerful the human brain is and how it functions while reading, it's time to get the speed reading ball rolling. And the first important step is to determine your current reading speed.

Why do this? It's because knowing and recording your reading speed will give you an objective basis for which to determine your progress. And based on the changes in your recorded reading speed, you can make the necessary adjustments if needed.

It's one thing to say, "I feel my reading speed has increased tremendously in the last 3 weeks." It's another to say, "In the last 3 weeks, I was able to increase my reading speed from 300 words-per-minute to 500 words-per-minute!"

Reading speed has 3 aspects: average speed, processing speed, and memorizing speed. Average speed refers to actual number of words you can read per minute, regardless if you're able to understand or memorize the things you read. Here's how to measure your average speed (AS):

1) Choose a page from a book or a specific reading material or use the text provided at the end of this chapter (word count is provided next to text).

2) Count the number of words of that page or reading material.

3) Using a timer, record how long it takes you to finish reading your chosen material.

4) Divide the number of words of your chosen reading material by the number of seconds it took you to finish reading it and multiply it by 60 to get your AS, expressed as words-per-minute (WPM).

The second aspect of reading speed is comprehension, which is measured as processing speed or (PS). While the goal of speed reading is to read fast, it won't mean much if you're not able to really make sense of what you have read. Measuring PS requires answering a set of questions after reading a piece of text, which are prepared by someone else to ensure integrity of questions. The proportion of questions answered correctly will determine the PS score, i.e., 8 out of 10 questions answered correctly means a PS score of 80%. Obviously you may not have someone to do this so you can simply think about what you just read and give a quick description of it to yourself. How easy you find this will determine your comprehension.

The final aspect of reading speed is memorizing speed (MS), which refers to how many words you can read and comprehend every minute. It's basically a combination of the AS (reading speed) and PS (comprehension).

MS is computed by multiplying the AS by the PS. If your AS is 300 WPM and your PS is 80%, then your MS is:

$$300 \text{ wpm} \times 80\% = 240 \text{ WPM}$$

The ultimate goal of speed reading is both speed and comprehension. That's why as much as possible, you should use MS as your barometer for speed reading improvement. However, it may be challenging or most inconvenient to measure progress with MS as it requires the help of another person to create questions to be performed correctly by which to measure your PS. Also, comprehension is a topic that can take another entire book to cover. Therefore, this book will focus mainly on AS.

To measure your baseline AS, read the following text, time yourself, and calculate your AS.

Treasure Island — Robert Louis Stevenson — (605 Words)

As soon as Silver disappeared, the captain, who had been closely watching him, turned toward the interior of the house and found not a man of us at his post but Gray. It was the first time we had ever seen him angry.

"Quarters!" he roared. And then, as we slunk back to our places, "Gray," he said, "I'll put your name in the log; you've stood by your duty like a seaman. Mr. Trelawney, I'm surprised at you, sir. Doctor, I thought you had worn the king's coat! If that was how you served at Fontenoy, sir, you'd have been better in your berth."

The doctor's watch were all back at their loopholes, the rest were busy loading the spare muskets, and everyone with a red face, you may be certain, and a flea in his ear, as the saying is.

The captain looked on for a while in silence. Then he spoke.

"My lads," he said, "I've given Silver a broadside. I pitched it in red-hot on purpose; and before the hour's out, as he said, we shall be boarded. We're outnumbered, I needn't tell you that, but we fight in shelter; and, a minute ago, I should have said we fought with discipline. I've no manner of doubt that we can drub them if you choose."

Then he went the rounds, and saw, as he said, that all was clear.

On the two short sides of the house, east and west, there were only two loopholes; on the south side where the porch was, two again; and on the north side, five. There was a round score of muskets for the seven of us; the firewood had been built into four piles—tables, you might say—one about the middle of each side, and on each of these tables some ammunition and four loaded muskets were laid ready to the hand of the defenders. In the middle, the cutlasses lay ranged.

"Toss out the fire," said the captain; "the chill is past, and we mustn't have smoke in our eyes."

The iron fire basket was carried bodily out by Mr. Trelawney, and the embers smothered among sand.

"Hawkins hasn't had his breakfast. Hawkins, help yourself, and back to your post to eat it," continued Captain Smollett. "Lively, now, my lad; you'll want it before you've done. Hunter, serve out a round of brandy to all hands."

And while this was going on the captain completed, in his own mind, the plan of the defense.

"Doctor, you will take the door," he resumed. "See and don't expose yourself; keep within, and fire through the porch. Hunter, take the east side, there. Joyce, you stand by the west, my man. Mr. Trelawney, you are the best shot—you and Gray will take this long north side, with the five loopholes; it's where the danger is. If they can get up to it, and fire in upon us through our own ports, things would begin to look dirty. Hawkins, neither you nor I are much account at the shooting; we'll stand by to load and bear a hand."

As the captain had said, the chill was past. As soon as the sun had climbed above our girdle of trees, it fell with all its force upon the clearing and drank up the vapors at a draught. Soon the sand was baking, and the resin melting in the logs of the blockhouse. Jackets and coats were flung aside;

shirts were thrown open at the neck and rolled up to the shoulders; and we stood there, each at his post, in a fever of heat and anxiety.

Chapter 4: Peripheral Vision

One of the most important aspects of speed reading is peripheral vision.

Basically, peripheral vision refers to your range of sight from one side of your vision to the other, i.e., the area of your vision beyond the middle of your gaze. It represents the greatest area of your visual field and the wider your peripheral vision is, the more things you can see in one glance.

Peripheral vision has 3 parts:

1) **Near-Peripheral Vision**, i.e., what you see adjacent to the middle of your gaze;

2) **Mid-Peripheral Vision**, i.e., what you see at the center of your visual field; and

3) **Far-Peripheral Vision**, i.e., what you see at the edge of your visual field.

A great chunk of improving reading speed is increasing peripheral reading vision, i.e., the number of words you can see in a fixed gaze. The more words you can see per gaze, the more words you'll be able to read. And the more words you can read for the same period of time, the faster you can read.

You can find plenty of peripheral vision improvement exercises online and it is definitely worth improving. I have include a few here for you to have a go at.

Peripheral Vision Improvement Exercise #1

1) Center your gaze on the star in the middle of the Picture 1-A below. Beginning with the letter "R," try and read the letters surrounding the star without taking your gaze away from it.

2) Perform this exercise up to 5 times per session, once or twice daily. Give your eyes time to rest before doing this exercise again.

3) Move on to Picture 1-B once you're able to recognize each letter easily. Then to Picture 1-C

Picture 1-A

Picture 1-B

Picture 1-C

Peripheral Vision Improvement Exercise #2

This exercise was designed to improve the flexibility of your eye muscle, which can translate into wider peripheral reading vision over time.

1) Begin by either standing or sitting down and focusing your sight straight in front of you.

2) Stretch out both hands to your sides, like you're creating a cross with your body. Your arms should be straight and perpendicular to the ground.

3) Make a thumbs-up sign with each hand and hold the pose for the duration of the exercise.

4) Keeping your head fixed and facing straight ahead of you, move your eyes to the right until you can see your right thumb. If your eye muscle isn't that flexible yet, just move it as far to the right as you can.

5) Move your eyes all the way to the left until you see your left thumb or as far as you can do it. That's one repetition. Perform 9 more times to complete 1 set of 10 repetitions.

6) Do 3 sets of this exercise per session and always remember to keep your head fixed and facing straight ahead throughout the movements.

Chapter 5: Important Speed Reading Principles

Now that you know how to improve your peripheral vision for speed reading, it's time to learn some of the most important principles for optimizing your reading speed. While these aren't the speed reading techniques or methods per se, they certainly help you make the most out of the techniques you'll learn in the next chapter.

Minimize Sub-Vocalization

Also called auditory reassurance, it's one of the most prevalent reading habits around. When a person sub-vocalizes, that person mentally pronounces or says the words being read. And this habit is one of the biggest stumbling blocks to optimizing reading speed. This alone helped my reading speed tremendously.

Most – if not all – speed reading programs claim to teach how to completely eliminate reading sub-vocalization as one of their top reading speed improvement tactics. But scientific studies have shown that's impossible to completely eliminate this habit. What is possible is substantially reducing this habit or minimizing it, which is still very helpful in terms of improving reading speed. Here are some practical ways you can minimize your tendency to sub-vocalize:

1) **Guide Your Eyes:** One of the foundational practices of effective speed reading is using something, e.g., a finger or an object, to guide the eyes while reading. This may seem a little juvenile but it works.

2) **Distractions:** One way to keep your mind from mentally pronouncing the things you read is by distracting it. However, the distraction shouldn't be that big or strong that it keeps you from actually reading! A very good way of distracting your mind enough to minimize sub-vocalization without distracting you from reading is to chew gum as you're reading. Again, very simple but this has worked for many people and is worth a try.

3) **Play Music:** For me, a better distraction than gum is music. With music in the background, the tendency to sub-vocalize can be reduced greatly. It can also help you concentrate better on what you're reading. Just make sure you avoid listening to music that has lyrics being sung, instrumental versions of songs with lyrics that you know, and music that has a very strong emotional resonance with you. Personally, I find that soft, classical music works best because it's not emotionally strong, it's calm, it usually has no lyrics, and isn't mainstream enough to distract my mind from actually reading. I still do this now whenever I read

4) **Just Read Faster:** By significantly increasing the pace at which you read, you can minimize the tendency to sub-vocalize. How? By giving your mind a much harder time to catch up with sub-vocalization. Reading significantly faster than you normally do can also help you focus better because faster reading requires heightened focus and attention.

Control Your Eye Movement

Ideally, eye movements while reading a book or some other reading material should have the same automatic responses as when typing an email or riding a bike in a busy street. By improving eye movement in a particular way, you can minimize the number of times your eyes stop when reading a line and the length or duration of each stop.

Why is it important to train the eye to move in specific ways for optimal reading speed? It's because eye movements impact our ability to read, including the speed at which we can read.

Take for example the fact that most people believe and claim that when they read, their eyes simply follow the print from side to side at a fairly consistent speed across pages. But the truth is, scientific studies have shown that the eyes tend to stop and go at several points in a line of text, i.e., fixation, in a jerky motion instead of flowing smoothly from side to side.

When our eyes move as we read, they're not really "looking" at individual words but rather, they just move from one stop or fixation point to another. And when it comes to the length of time spent reading every line of text, eye movements only account for 10% of the duration. What this means is reading a line of text is made up of several stops-and-goes or individual glances as well as making sense of each glance.

When it comes to eye movement and reading speed, you must keep this very important principle in mind: the more fixations or stops-and-goes are made when reading a line of text, the time needed to make sense of each fixation increases too. Longer duration plus higher frequency equals longer reading time, i.e., slower reading speed. This is why your peripheral vision is so important as less fixations will be required.

However, the ideal number of fixations per line of text and the duration of each fixation shouldn't be a one-size-fits-all proposition. These would depend on the reading difficulty or ease of the reading material. It's only natural to take longer to process unfamiliar or very technical reading materials, hence a slower reading speed.

The primary purpose for reading specific texts should also be major considerations of reading speed. Reading an audited financial report for purposes of investing a huge sum of money in the stocks of a New York Stock Exchange-listed company should take much more time compared to reading Dan Brown's bestselling novel The Da Vinci Code.

Minimize Regression

Regression refers to the reading habit of frequently going back to texts you already read just to ensure that you really understood it. As you can see, frequently going back to parts of a text you've already read will slow down your reading speed because of frequent repetitions. Until learning of regression when reading, I didn't realise just how much I actually did this.

There are two ways you can minimize your tendency to regress while reading. First, you must prime yourself up to focus and read for a specific period of time. This involves committing or blocking off time for reading, i.e., cutting yourself off from all possible reading distractions like social media, email, or communications with other people. When you get distracted, you get thrown off from what you're reading, which will compel you to retrace your reading "steps" just to get back into the flow.

Second, you can use something to cover the lines you've already read as you move down to the bottom of the page you're reading. This can be a piece of white paper folded crosswise, which you can place on top of a book or a page of material you're reading. As you finish reading one line after another, slide that folded paper on top of the lines you already read to prevent yourself from regressing. Do the same for succeeding pages you'll read. You wont have to do this for long to train yourself out of regressing.

Here's a good exercise for developing the habit of minimizing regression:

1) Choose a physical book to read, which should neither be important or complex to read. A novel is a good example of such a book.

2) Block off at least 30 minutes every day to do this exercise without any distractions or disruptions. This should be the only thing you'll focus on for 30 minutes.

3) In your mind, commit to completely focus on the exercise and not regressing to any previously finished texts or lines.

4) Use a white sheet of paper folded cross-wise to cover lines you've already read while moving down each page of the book you chose to read.

The Chunking Method

Also called chunk reading, chunking is a reading principle which says that the best way to make sense of texts is by chunking or grouping them together. This is consistent with the fact that we don't read "words" per se but clusters of words.

For example, which is easier to read and understand between these two? Option A:

Stephen

Curry

Nailed

A

Killer

Crossover

Punctuated

By

A

30-foot

3-point

Shot.

Or Option B, which chunks words together as indicated by the symbol |:

Stephen Curry | nailed a killer cross-over |
punctuated by | a 30-foot 3-point shot.

Of course, Option B is the easier version to read and make sense of, right? Right!

Learning to Chunk Read Better

If this is the first time you've heard of or learned about chunking, start by learning how to "triple-chunk" first. Here's how to do it:

1) Start by choosing a page of printed text and dividing it into 3 parts by drawing 2 vertical lines on the page to demarcate each of the equally-sized sections. The first line should cut off the first 2 words of each line while the second line should cut off the last two words of each line.

2) Focus your eyes on the middle section of the page only and just let your peripheral vision see the first 2 and the last 2 words of the line.

3) Focus only on reading the text in between the 2 lines, i.e., the middle section. Don't mind the outer edges.

Once you've mastered the triple-chunking principle, the next principle to master is the double-chunking one. Here's how to practice it:

1) Divide a page of text into 2 equal halves by drawing a vertical line through the middle.

2) Read through the page line by line. Do this by glancing once on each side of the line, treating each half as if a whole unit.

3) With continuous practice, you'll learn to focus on the middle line only and be able to read entire lines via a wider peripheral reading vision.

Chapter 6: Speed Reading Techniques

Now, let's get to the meat of speed reading. In this chapter, we'll cover the primary techniques you can learn to use to optimize your reading speed.

The Skimming and Scanning Method

These refer to reading techniques that utilize REM or rapid eye movements (no your not going to have a nap) together with keywords. The primary objective of these 2 techniques is to move quickly through written texts by identifying keywords that reveal the key ideas or points of a text.

What's the difference between the 2? Skimming is rapid reading the objective of which is to provide you with a general overview of what you're reading, i.e., general ideas or points. Scanning refers to rapid reading, the objective of which is to give you specific facts.

Skimming gives you an idea of the general information or ideas within specific sections while scanning gives you specific facts or ideas. To use a more familiar comparison, skimming is snorkeling while scanning is diving.

When should you skim and when should you scan? You can use skimming for:

1) Reading before reading a material, i.e., previewing a particular material;

2) Reading after reading a material, i.e., reviewing a particular material;

3) Getting the main idea from a long reading material you neither have the desire nor the time to read extensively; or

4) Finding resource materials for a research paper, an article you're writing, or a book you're planning to publish.

Scanning is more appropriate when you're:

1) Looking for specific facts during research;

2) Studying topics that are filled to the brim with facts; or

3) To provide factual support in answering questions that require it.

How to Skim Read

You must prepare yourself to rapidly move through pages when attempting to skim. You won't read each and every word in the text, but you will need to focus on typographical indicators like:

1) Numbered lists;

2) Bulleted lists;

3) Indented words or paragraphs;

4) Bold-lettered or italicized words; and

5) Headings.

When skimming, you must be on the lookout for unfamiliar words, names of places and people, nouns, dates, and keywords and phrases.

Here are the steps to follow to learn how to skim-read:

1) To get a general idea of how a reading material's main ideas or divided and sub-divided, go through the chapter overview (if any) or the table of contents.

2) Take quick look at each of the chapter's main headings or each main heading's sub-headings to get clues on what they're about. You can also read the headings of tables and charts if provided.

3) Read the whole opening paragraph of each chapter or main section of the text you're reading.

4) Then, read only the first and last sentences of each succeeding paragraph.

5) For every succeeding paragraph, just read the first few words of each sentence therein or look for the paragraph's main idea only.

6) Stop and read the boldfaced or italicized sentences with keywords very quickly.

7) If you believe that you've stumbled on a very important idea, stop skimming and read the whole sentence to verify your hunch. Afterward, return to skim-reading.

8) Where there are chapter or main section summaries, read them.

Ideally, you should go through all the above-mentioned steps. However, nobody's perfect and we don't live in a perfect world, i.e., there will be times it's not possible to do so. When that happens, just compromise by focusing only on the chapter overviews and summaries or other available indicators like boldfaced or italicized words, etc. Sometimes, the main ideas inside paragraphs aren't always in the last and first sentences so you'll have to make do with what's available like a chapter or section summary or overview.

Skimming is definitely a much faster way to read through materials, it doesn't have to be done at the same speed. There are certain sections of text where you'll need to slow down your skim-reading, such as:

1) Skimming through introducing and concluding paragraphs;

2) Skimming through topic sentences;

3) When you encounter an unfamiliar word; and

4) When reading a very complicated material.

How to Scan

Just like skimming, scanning involves keywords and typographical indicators. The difference lies in the objective, i.e., scanning isn't concerned about getting a bird's eye view of a material but with finding and getting specific facts or information. Often times, scanning is the next step after skimming through materials as skimming helps provide a general roadmap for a guided scan.

Here are the practical steps for learning how to scan:

1) Identify what it is you're looking for. Choose specific search terms like keywords or keyword phrases. When you scan, you'll be a human-equivalent of Google and other search engines.

2) When scanning, focus on finding one search term at a time. If you have several search

terms, scan the material multiple times per the number of your search terms.

3) Allow your eyes to float down pages quickly until you're able to locate your specific search term.

4) As soon as your eyes locate any of your keywords or phrases, read the texts immediately preceding and following it to get an idea of its context and check for relevancy.

If you want to scan materials with the objective of finding factual support for answering questions, it can be easier because one important aspect of scanning's already been done for you. Questions – by nature – already provide the keywords you'll need for scanning. The remaining steps for scanning in order to answer specific questions include:

1) Thoroughly read the questions prior to scanning your materials. From the questions themselves, you can identify your scanning keywords.

2) If you have multiple questions to answer, scan for answers for one question at a time. Each scan must focus on answers to one question only.

3) As soon as you find a keyword or phrase, check the texts immediately preceding and

succeeding that keyword or phrase to check for relevancy.

4) Read the questions again to know if the answers you discover are appropriate for answering your questions.

You can practice skimming and scanning on this text:

Read the following 2 questions and see if you can quickly answer them by skimming and scanning:

1) Which century did the Magyars conquer the country?

2) What was the dream about?

Once you have answered the previous questions. There are 2 more after the text. Skim and scan the entire text before reading these and see if you can answer them.

Dracula – Bram Stoker – (605 Words)

In the population of Transylvania there are four distinct nationalities: Saxons in the South, and mixed with them the Wallachs, who are the descendants of the Dacians; Magyars in the West, and Szekelys in the East and North. I am going among the latter, who claim to be descended from Attila and the Huns. This may be so, for when the Magyars conquered the country in the eleventh century they found the Huns settled in it. I read that every known superstition in the world is gathered into the horseshoe of the Carpathians as if it were the center of some sort of imaginative whirlpool; if so my stay may be very interesting. (Mem., I must ask the Count all about them.)

I did not sleep well, though my bed was comfortable enough, for I had all sorts of queer dreams. There was a dog howling all night under my window, which may have had something to do with it; or it may have been the paprika, for I had to drink up all the water in my carafe, and was still thirsty. Towards morning I slept and was wakened by the continuous knocking at my door, so I guess I must have been sleeping soundly then. I had for breakfast more paprika, and a sort of porridge of maize flour which they said was "mamaliga," and egg-plant stuffed with forcemeat, a very excellent dish, which they call "impletata." (Mem., get recipe for this also.) I had to hurry breakfast, for the train started a little before eight, or rather it ought to have done so, for after rushing to the station at 7:30 I had to sit in the carriage for more than an hour before we began to move. It seems to me that the further east you go the more unpunctual are the trains. What ought they to be in China?

All day long we seemed to dawdle through a country which was full of beauty of every kind. Sometimes we saw little towns or castles on the top of steep hills such as we see in old missals; sometimes we ran by rivers and streams which seemed from the wide stony margin on each side of them to be subject to great floods. It takes a lot of water and running strong, to sweep the outside edge of a river clear. At every station there were groups of people, sometimes crowds, and in all sorts of attire. Some of them were just like the peasants at home or those I saw coming through France and Germany, with short jackets and round hats and home-made trousers; but others were very picturesque. The women looked pretty, except when you got near them, but they were very clumsy about the waist. They had all full white sleeves of some kind or other, and most of them had big belts with a lot of strips of something fluttering from them like the dresses in a ballet, but of course there were petticoats under them. The strangest figures we saw were the Slovaks, who were more barbarian than the rest, with their big cowboy hats, great baggy dirty-white trousers, white linen shirts, and enormous heavy leather belts, nearly a foot wide, all studded over with brass nails. They wore high boots, with their trousers tucked into them, and had long black hair and heavy black mustaches. They are very picturesque, but do not look prepossessing. On the stage they would be set down at once as some old

Oriental band of brigands. They are, however, I am told, very harmless and rather wanting in natural self-assertion.

3) What time did they arrive at the train station?

4) What hats did the Slovaks wear?

The Meta Guiding (Tracker and Pacer) Method

This refers to one of the most established speed reading techniques, which I suspect you're already familiar with after reading through this book. Meta-guiding is a simple reading technique that involves using an object, e.g., your finger, the tip of a covered pen, etc., to trace below the certain texts you are reading, which act as specific fixation points consistent with chunking. Such an object serves as a tracker or pacer for your eyes when reading across written texts.

The primary principle of meta-guiding for speed reading is to move your pacing and tracking object (finger, pen, etc.) at a pace that's faster than your regular reading speed. Because the object is meant to guide your eyes as you read, doing so will force your eyes to "catch up" to the faster than usual pace. Over time, your eyes can get used to the faster pace, resulting in a significantly faster average reading speed.

The primary reason why meta-guiding is effective in helping people who practice it consistently read faster is because it minimizes the habit of regression. If you remember correctly from our earlier discussion, regression is the habit of going back to re-read texts you've already read.

Just to refresh your memory, regression is one of the worst reading habits a person can have because for one, it means that person isn't reading well enough to the point that he or she has to go back to the text just to understand it. And as you remember, going back effectively doubles reading time for the re-read texts and if this happens frequently, it can result in slow reading speed. Meta-guiding can help you improve your reading speed by making sure that you read every line only once, which ensures continuous progress through the materials you're reading.

Meta guiding is also very easy to practice! You just need your finger to do it!

1) Begin by using your finger, pen, stylus or whatever contraption to run beneath specific texts (fixation points) on the line you're reading at a speed that's just slightly faster than your normal reading speed. Depending on your current chunking ability, it may be 2, 3 or 4 fixation or stop points per line.

2) When you're done with the first line, read the next by running your tracker or pacer through each of your line's fixation points at the same speed.

3) Gradually increase the speed at which you move your tracking contraption as you read.

Over time, your eyes will be able to read significantly faster than today.

You can practice meta-guiding on this text and remember, no regression and no sub-vocalizing. Keep your tracker moving at a consistent pace:

Toto came up, and immediately began to bark, but Dorothy made him be still.

The Lion climbed the ladder next, and the Tin Woodman came last; but both of them cried, "Oh, my!" as soon as they looked over the wall. When they were all sitting in a row on the top of the wall, they looked down and saw a strange sight.

Before them was a great stretch of country having a floor as smooth and shining and white as the bottom of a big platter. Scattered around were many houses made entirely of china and painted in the brightest colors. These houses were quite small, the biggest of them reaching only as high as Dorothy's waist. There were also pretty little barns, with china fences around them; and many cows and sheep and horses and pigs and chickens, all made of china, were standing about in groups.

But the strangest of all were the people who lived in this queer country. There were milkmaids and shepherdesses, with brightly colored bodices and golden spots all over their gowns; and princesses with most gorgeous frocks of silver and gold and purple; and shepherds dressed in knee breeches with pink and yellow and blue stripes down them, and golden buckles on their shoes; and princes with jeweled crowns upon their heads, wearing ermine robes and satin doublets; and funny clowns in ruffled gowns, with round red spots upon their cheeks and tall, pointed caps. And, strangest of all, these people were all made of china, even to their clothes, and were so small that the tallest of them was no higher than Dorothy's knee.

No one did so much as look at the travelers at first, except one little purple china dog with an extra-large head, which came to the wall and barked at them in a tiny voice, afterward running away again. "How shall we get down?" asked Dorothy.

They found the ladder so heavy they could not pull it up, so the Scarecrow fell off the wall and the others jumped down upon him so that the hard floor would not hurt their feet. Of course they took pains not to light on his head and get the pins in their feet. When all were safely down they picked up the Scarecrow, whose body was quite flattened out, and patted his straw into shape again.

"We must cross this strange place in order to get to the other side," said Dorothy, "for it would be unwise for us to go any other way except due South."

They began walking through the country of the china people, and the first thing they came to was a china milkmaid milking a china cow. As they drew near, the cow suddenly gave a kick and kicked over the stool, the pail, and even the milkmaid herself, and all fell on the china ground with a great clatter.

Dorothy was shocked to see that the cow had broken her leg off and that the pail was lying in several small pieces, while the poor milkmaid had a nick in her left elbow.

"There!" cried the milkmaid angrily. "See what you have done! My cow has broken her leg, and I must take her to the mender's shop and have it glued on again. What do you mean by coming here and frightening my cow?"

"I'm very sorry," returned Dorothy. "Please forgive us."

But the pretty milkmaid was much too vexed to make any answer. She picked up the leg sulkily and led her cow away, the poor animal limping on three legs. As she left them the milkmaid cast many reproachful glances over her shoulder at the clumsy strangers, holding her nicked elbow close to her side.

The Phrase Reading Technique

This technique can help you better comprehend what you read, improve your reading fluency, and strengthen your oral reading abilities. You can also use to improve your grammar, vocabulary, and punctuation.   Here's how to perform this technique:

Choose Your Reading

Choose the kind of reading you want to do, i.e., pleasure reading or reading to learn something?   If you're reading for pleasure, you don't have to read at a faster clip than necessary so you can really enjoy your reading time.   Take the time to appreciate the material's cadence and rhythms, choice of words, mental imageries, and concepts.   Pleasure reading should be like pleasure eating, i.e., not hurried.

If you're reading to learn, especially if you're under time limits, you must focus on understanding the material and more importantly, understand it in the least amount of time.   You'll have to do speed reading for this kind of learning.

Quick Glances

When you start reading, don't stare at words but quickly glance through phrases.   Further, don't even think or say the words but concentrate on glancing at phrases and figuring out what they mean. Picture the meaning of the phrase as quickly as you can in your mind.

Again, you must practice the principle of chunking words into phrases. Don't read one word at a time.

Imagine or Visualize Every Phrase

This may take some effort and time in the beginning because chances are, this isn't something you're already doing. But think about it, reading words as groups of letters didn't come naturally to you at first too. With enough practice, you can learn to read by phrases or word chunks instead of per word.

Remember, words are just individual symbols that in and by themselves hardly provides meaningful thoughts. It's only when words are bunched together in phrases and sentences that they're able to express unique messages. That's why it only makes sense to imagine or visualize the meaning of phrases instead of individual words.

Don't Read Too Fast

Yes, speed reading involves reading at a significantly faster rate than normal. However, it doesn't mean over-speeding! Just like with driving, it's possible to over-speed when it comes to reading.

How do you know when your over-speed reading? The primary indicator is that you're unable to get the meaning of the phrases you're reading. Remember, the primary goal of speed reading is to read and comprehend more materials within the same length of time. Neither comprehending at a very slow speed nor reading a lot of material that can't be understood is the essence of speed reading.

When using the phrase-reading technique to speed read, you should be able to read as fast as possible but still being able to understand the meaning of the phrases you're reading. If you focus primarily on reading phrases faster, comprehension may be compromised. But if you prioritize learning how to get the meaning out of phrases, speed will eventually follow.

This method is essentially the chunking method but has been laid out slightly different. You can try this technique on the following text which has been separated into chunks via different colours. Read only the grey text and let you eyes skim over the black:

Oliver Twist – Charles Dickens – (601 Words)

For the next eight or ten months, Oliver was the victim of a systematic course of treachery and deception. He was brought up by hand. The hungry and destitute situation of the infant orphan was duly reported by the workhouse authorities to the parish authorities. The parish authorities inquired with dignity of the workhouse authorities, whether there was no female then domiciled in 'the house' who was in a situation to impart to Oliver Twist, the consolation and nourishment of which he stood in need. The workhouse authorities replied with humility that there was not. Upon this, the parish authorities magnanimously and humanely resolved, that Oliver should be 'farmed,' or, in other words, that he should be dispatched to a branch-workhouse some three miles off, where twenty or thirty other juvenile offenders against the poor-laws, rolled about the floor all day, without the inconvenience of too much food or too much clothing, under the parental superintendence of an elderly female, who received the culprits at and for the consideration of seven pence-halfpenny per small head per week. Seven pence-halfpenny's worth per week is a good round diet for a child; a great deal may be got for seven pence-halfpenny, quite enough to overload its stomach and make it uncomfortable. The elderly female was a woman of wisdom and experience; she knew what was good for children; and she had a very accurate perception of what was good for herself. So, she appropriated the greater part of the weekly stipend to her own use and consigned the rising *parochial* generation to even a **shorter allowance than was** originally provided **for them. Thereby finding** in the lowest depth **a deeper still; and** proving herself **a very great** experimental **philosopher.**

Everybody knows the story **of another experimental** philosopher who **had a great theory about** a horse being able **to live without eating,** and who demonstrated **it so well, that** he had got his own horse **down to a straw a** day, and would **unquestionably have rendered** him a very spirited **and rampacious animal** on nothing at all, **if he had not died,** four-and-twenty hours **before he was to have** had his first comfortable **bait of air.** Unfortunately for, the **experimental philosophy of** the female to whose **protecting care Oliver** Twist was delivered **over, a similar result** usually attended the **operation of her system;** for at the very moment **when the child had** contrived to exist **upon the smallest** possible portion of the **weakest possible food, it** did perversely happen **in eight and a** half cases out of ten, **either that it sickened from** want and cold, or fell **into the fire from** neglect, or got **half-smothered by accident;** in any one of which **cases, the miserable** little being was usually **summoned into another** world, and there **gathered to the** fathers it had never **known in this.**

Occasionally, when there was **some more than** usually interesting inquest **upon a parish child** who had been **overlooked in turning** up a bedstead, or **inadvertently scalded to** death when there **happened to be a washing—**though the latter **accident was very scarce,** anything approaching **to a washing being** of rare occurrence in **the farm —the jury** would take it into **their heads to ask**

troublesome questions, **or the parishioners** *would* *rebelliously* **affix their signatures** *to a remonstrance*. **But these impertinences** *were speedily checked* **by the evidence of** *the surgeon,* *and* **the testimony of the beadle;** *the former of whom* **had always opened** *the body and* **found nothing inside (which** *was very probable* **indeed), and the latter** *of whom invariably* **swore whatever** *the parish* **wanted; which** *was very* **self-devotional.**

Know What's Best for Your Comprehension

Each person is different. That being said, each person can also benefit differently from different speed reading techniques. If you want to optimize your reading speed, try out one speed reading technique every one or two weeks and record improvements – or lack thereof – in your average reading speed. That's the only way you can objectively determine which technique is best for your reading speed and comprehension.

Chapter 7: Reading Comprehension Tips

I'll never get tired of emphasizing the primary goal of speed reading, which is to optimize reading speed without compromising reading comprehension. Again, speed reading without comprehension is worthless while reading comprehension may not mean much if it takes forever to achieve.

But what does reading comprehension really mean? It refers to the ability to understand what is read. It's an active, intentional, and interactive endeavor that a person undertakes before, during and after reading a particular material.

With poor reading comprehension, speed reading – or reading for that matter – is nothing more than just looking at and sounding off various symbols. Think of an American who only knows how to read and speak American English trying to read an ancient Chinese scroll from the Ming Dynasty. He may be able to appreciate the aesthetic parts of the scroll's text, but he or she will never be able to really understand what the scroll is saying. For that person, the scroll is meaningless and possibly worthless because all it contains are unintelligible symbols.

More importantly, functional literacy is dependent on good reading comprehension skills. In today's highly competitive world, people need to be able to quickly learn new skills and abilities in order to survive economically. Without adequate reading comprehension skills, it'll be impossible to grow in skills and knowledge and consequently, survive economically.

The SQ3R Method

This is one of the most popular and effective methods for developing reading comprehension. SQ3R stands for:

- **S** is for Survey;
- **Q** stands for Question; and
- **3R** stands for Read, Recite, and Review.

Here's how to employ the SQ3R method for improving reading comprehension:

Survey

Before reading a chapter or main section of a reading material, survey it first by looking at the following:

1) The title, the main headings and their sub-headings;

2) Any captions provided for maps, charts, graphs, and pictures;

3) Any available study guides or questions;

4) Introducing and concluding paragraphs; and

5) Summaries.

Question

While you're surveying the material, ask questions by, among others:

1) Converting the titles, main headings and subheadings into inquiries or questions;

2) Reading questions at the end of each chapter, main heading or sub-heading, if any are provided; or

3) Asking yourself what you already know about the topic covered by the material.

Read

While you're reading the material:

1) Try to answer the questions you initially raised during the Question portion;

2) If there are any questions provided at the start or end of the chapter or main section, answer them.

3) If there are any captions provided for featured graphics, pictures, charts or tables, read them again;

4) Take note of any words or phrases that were boldfaced, italicized, or underlined for emphasis by the author;

5) When you come across relatively challenging parts, slow down your reading speed;

6) I know I said no regression when reading but for portions of the text that you feel aren't clear, stop and re-read them if you feel they are particularly important; and

Recite

1) Read one section, chapter or paragraph at a time and recite what you understood to be its main points or ideas;

2) Orally summarize the material you read in your own words;

3) After speed reading through the material, re-read and take notes from the material, writing them down in your own words;

4) Highlight or underline the important points you come across with; and

5) Recite!

Review

The review process is fairly simple: just re-speed read your material that's already highlighted with notes taken.

Try this out on an old book you have or a report you wish to understand more thoroughly.

Chapter 8: Calculating Your New Reading Speed

As mentioned earlier, the best way to monitor your speed reading progress is by measuring your actual reading speed, recording them, and comparing your current speed with the previous ones. After giving a particular speed reading technique a try for 7 to 14 days, measure your AS or average reading speed. If you recall, the AS is all about pure reading speed and doesn't check for comprehension. And to remind you how to measure it:

1) Choose a page from a book or a specific reading material.

2) Count the number of words of that page or reading material.

3) Using a timer, record how long it takes you to finish reading your chosen material.

4) Divide the number of words of your chosen reading material by the number of seconds it took you to finish reading it and multiply it by 60 to get your AS, expressed as words-per-minute (WPM).

If you record a higher reading WPM after 7 to 14 days of using a specific technique, it means it's working for you. If you're happy with the progress, you can choose to continue using the technique. If you're not happy with the increase or if your registered new WPM is lower, you can use another technique for another 7 to 14 days and re-measure your reading speed again. And when you do, use this text:

The War of the Worlds – H. G. Wells – (601 Words)

The most extraordinary thing to my mind, of all the strange and wonderful things that happened upon that Friday, was the dovetailing of the commonplace habits of our social order with the first beginnings of the series of events that was to topple that social order headlong. If on Friday night you had taken a pair of compasses and drawn a circle with a radius of five miles around the Woking sand-pits, I doubt if you would have had one human being outside it, unless it were some relation of Stent or of the three or four cyclists or London people lying dead on the common, whose emotions or habits were at all affected by the new-comers. Many people had heard of the cylinder, of course, and talked about it in their leisure, but it certainly did not make the sensation that an ultimatum to Germany would have done.

In London that night poor Henderson's telegram describing the gradual unscrewing of the shot was judged to be a canard, and his evening paper, after wiring for authentication from him and receiving no reply—the man was killed—decided not to print a special edition.

Even within the five-mile circle the great majority of people were inert. I have already described the behavior of the men and women to whom I spoke. All over the district people were dining and supping; working men were gardening after the labors of the day, children were being put to bed, young people were wandering through the lanes love-making, students sat over their books.

Maybe there was a murmur in the village streets, a novel and dominant topic in the public-houses, and here and there a messenger, or even an eye-witness of the later occurrences, caused a whirl of excitement, a shouting, and a running to and fro; but for the most part the daily routine of working, eating, drinking, sleeping, went on as it had done for countless years—as though no planet Mars existed in the sky. Even at Woking station and Horsell and Chobham that was the case.

In Woking junction, until a late hour, trains were stopping and going on, others were shunting on the sidings, passengers were alighting and waiting, and everything was proceeding in the most ordinary way. A boy from the town, trenching on Smith's monopoly, was selling papers with the afternoon's news. The ringing impact of trucks, the sharp whistle of the engines from the junction, mingled with their shouts of "Men from Mars!" Excited men came into the station about nine o'clock with incredible tidings, and caused no more disturbance than drunkards might have done. People rattling Londonwards peered into the darkness outside the carriage windows, and saw only a rare, flickering, vanishing spark dance up from the direction of Horsell, a red glow and a thin veil of smoke driving across the stars, and thought that nothing more serious than a heath fire was happening. It was only around the edge of the common that any disturbance was perceptible. There were half a dozen villas burning on the Woking border. There were lights in all the houses on the common side of the three villages, and the people there kept awake till dawn.

A curious crowd lingered restlessly, people coming and going but the crowd remaining, both on the Chobham and Horsell bridges. One or two adventurous souls, it was afterward found, went into the darkness and crawled quite near the Martians; but they never returned, for now and again a light-ray, like the beam of a warship's searchlight swept the common, and the Heat-Ray was ready to follow.

So, whats your new AS or WPM? Remember, numbers don't lie! That's why measuring or calculating your new reading speed is important for accurately monitoring your speed reading progress.

Chapter 9: External and Internal Reading Optimizers

While speed reading techniques are the primary means by which you can greatly improve the rate at which you read, it doesn't mean it's complete. There are 2 non-reading things you can do that can supplement your speed reading techniques and give you that extra speed reading edge.

These are some more "Captain Obvious" statements here but I had to include them as they really do make a huge difference and it's a good idea to keep them in mind.

Your Reading Environment

If you read in a very noisy or uncomfortable environment, you'll be too distracted to read optimally, regardless of speed. Your reading environment will have a huge impact on your ability to focus on what you're reading and more importantly, on your ability to understand what you're reading.

Some of the most important things you're reading environment must have include:

1) Adequate Lighting: Soft or dim lights can make you feel too relaxed to focus. Too

much lighting can also lead to physical discomforts such as eye strain or headaches.

2) Quiet: Even if you're reading in an adequately lit place, a noisy environment will surely distract you or at the very least, prevent you from reading optimally.

3) Privacy: If you're reading in an environment where people can easily disturb you, your chances of being able to focus on your reading is practically zero. That's why unless you live alone or have a room in your house where you can lock yourself to read without being interrupted, it'll be better to go to a well-lit coffee shop or the library instead.

4) The Right Temperature: It'll be hard to concentrate on reading – or any mental endeavor – if you're in an environment that's too hot or too cold. If it's too hot, you'll be sweating like a pig and get dehydrated. If it's too cold, you can feel very sluggish or sleepy and worse, may end up with a major headache.

Mental Focus

Without the ability to focus well, it's going to be very hard to practice speed reading. It'll be hard to even read normally. Effective reading requires concentration and focus and if the monkey brain remains untamed, both are impossible.

There are 2 ways you can focus on your reading efforts better: reading in the right environment as previously mentioned. And, regular meditation can actually help.   Your environment minimizes external distractions while if you choose, regular meditation can help minimize internal distractions.   Meditation can help improve control over your mind, particularly the ability to manage random thoughts and keep them at bay. Just something to think about.

Conclusion

Thanks for grabbing a copy of this book and more importantly, finishing reading it. Now that you're done reading it, you have enough information to start working on improving your reading speed. However, there's one thing that this book can't give you that can spell the difference between success and failure in your efforts to increase reading speed. And that's action.

You see, knowing is just half the battle and the other half is action. To be more specific, the other half is application of what is learned. Knowledge is just potential power and application is what unleashes the power.

So, I highly encourage you to start applying one of the speed reading techniques today on a daily basis for at least 1 week. That way, you give yourself enough time to increase your reading speed. If your first chosen technique doesn't give you satisfactory improvements, try another technique. Remember, Rome wasn't built in a day, but they were busy laying bricks by the hour. When it comes to significantly improving your reading speed, it'll take some time, too.

Here's to your speed reading success my friend! Cheers!

Note From The Author

I really hope you've enjoyed this book and its helped you towards your improving your reading speed. The most important thing is to practice. This isn't about becoming the best speed reader in history. Anyone can do this. So good luck my friend and again, thank you

Please go to Amazon.com to add a review.

References:

1. https://www.bustle.com/p/what-does-reading-do-to-your-brain-these-5-effects-are-pretty-astounding-74676
2. https://myspeedreading.com/how-the-brain-functions-while-speed-reading/
3. https://wonderopolis.org/wonder/how-do-we-remember
4. http://blogs.biomedcentral.com/bmcblog/2014/08/11/the-power-of-pictures-how-we-can-use-images-to-promote-and-communicate-science/
5. http://www.insanity-mind.com/measure-reading-speed/
6. http://www.readwritework.com/eye-exercises-improve-peripheral-vision/
7. https://www.irisreading.com/speed-reading-tips-5-ways-to-minimize-subvocalization/
8. https://blog.penningtonpublishing.com/reading/eye-movement-and-speed-reading/
9. http://www.insanity-mind.com/avoid-regression-speed-reading/
10. https://myspeedreading.com/read-group-of-words/
11. http://www.butte.edu/departments/cas/tipsheets/readingstrategies/skimming_scanning.html
12. https://www.how2become.com/blog/speed-reading-techniques/
13. https://www.wikihow.com/Read-Faster-by-Looking-at-Phrases
14. http://www.studygs.net/texred2.htm

15. https://www.k12reader.com/what-is-reading-comprehension/